## Solo Cello
### *Arranged and Edited by Joanne Martin*

## CONTENTS

Copyright © 1998 Summy-Birchard Music
division of Summy-Birchard Inc.
exclusively distributed by
Warner Bros. Publications
15800 N.W. 48th Avenue, Miami, FL 33014
All rights reserved     Printed in U.S.A.

ISBN: 0-87487-978-7

D1550981

# INTRODUCTION

The holiday season is a time of festive gatherings, and the music of this time of year is especially well-loved.  There are many opportunities to play with multi-generation family groups, as well as mixed-level studio and school ensembles.  *More Festive Strings*, like its companion volume *Festive Strings*, is a collection of well-known Christmas and Chanukah melodies in arrangements that have evolved to meet the needs of the individuals, groups, and orchestras I have taught.  In order to provide maximum flexibility, the arrangements are available in a number of instrumentations:

>
> ### *More Festive Strings for String Quartet or String Orchestra*
> | | |
> |---|---|
> | Appropriate for: | Suzuki students in Book 4 and beyond |
> | | Middle school or high school orchestras |
>
> ### *More Festive Strings for Violin Ensemble*
> ### *More Festive Strings for Viola Ensemble*
> ### *More Festive Strings for Cello Ensemble*
> For 2, 3, or 4 violin, viola, cello players in any combination of these instruments
> | | |
> |---|---|
> | Appropriate for: | Suzuki students in Book 4 and beyond |
> | | Middle school or high school orchestras |
>
> ### *More Festive Strings for Solo Violin*
> ### *More Festive Strings for Solo Viola*
> ### *More Festive Strings for Solo Cello*
> | | |
> |---|---|
> | For use with: | *More Festive Strings for String Quartet or String Orchestra* |
> | | *More Festive Strings for Violin, Viola, or Cello Ensemble* |
> | | *More Festive Strings Piano Accompaniments* |
> | Appropriate for players with 1–4 years of experience | |
>
> ### *More Festive Strings Piano Accompaniments*
> | | |
> |---|---|
> | For use with: | *More Festive Strings for String Quartet or String Orchestra* |
> | | *More Festive Strings for Violin, Viola, or Cello Ensemble* |
> | | *More Festive Strings for Solo Violin, Viola, or Cello* |
> | Appropriate for intermediate level pianists | |

Christmas and Chanukah tunes are popular with students at all levels, and even the youngest beginners enjoy taking part.  With this in mind, I have chosen the most accessible keys, which usually are the most resonant keys for string players.  Occasional compromises were necessary because of the differences between the violin, viola, and cello.

Introductions are optional and may be used at the discretion of the director or performers.

Shifting is kept to a minimum and finger numbers are normally used only to indicate the first note of a new position.  Occasionally, notes that remain in position are marked in parentheses.

These Solo Violin, Viola, and Cello parts duplicate the top part of *More Festive Strings for Violin, Viola,* or *Cello Ensemble*. They are intended for students in their first few years of playing, and may be learned by ear or by reading.  Beginning readers should find the single line of music and the slightly larger type easier to read than the score form used in the ensemble arrangements.

The solo parts also duplicate the melody, which is passed from voice to voice, in *More Festive Strings for String Quartet or String Orchestra* so that an individual or group of players can have orchestral accompaniment.

"Silent Night" appears in both G Major and D Major.  Violinists may prefer the D Major version, while violists and cellists may choose the G Major version.  Mixed ensembles can choose the key that best suits the abilities of the players.

During the preparation of this collection, many colleagues, friends, and students have played the arrangements, and their advice and detailed suggestions have been invaluable.  In particular I would like to thank Alex Adaman, Joanne and Charles Bath, Carey Cheney, Sally Gross, Eric Hansen, Carolyn Meyer, Rick Mooney, Karla Phillipp, Robert Richardson, Patricia Shand, Carol Tarr, and Ruth Wiwchar.  I am indebted to Fiona Shand for her careful work, perceptive proofreading, and cheerful sense of humor, and to my husband Peter for his unfailing encouragement and patience; both helped enormously in the completion of this volume.  *More Festive Strings* is dedicated to my parents, in gratitude for the love and music that enriched my childhood.

I hope that you enjoy *More Festive Strings* and that these arrangements contribute to your enjoyment of the holiday season.

Joanne Martin

# TEACHERS' NOTES

**O Chanukah**  All solo parts are in first position

**Angels We Have Heard on High**  Solo Violin and Solo Viola are in first position
Solo Cello shifts to E (second position)

**We Three Kings**  All solo parts are in first position

In *More Festive Strings for Violin, Viola,* or *Cello Ensemble; More Festive Strings for Solo Violin, Viola,* or *Cello;* and the *Piano Accompaniments,* "We Three Kings" has one verse with a repeat.

In *More Festive Strings for String Quartet* or *String Orchestra,* "We Three Kings" has two verses.

**Silent Night in D Major**  Solo Violin is in first position
Solo Viola shifts to G (third position)
Solo Cello shifts to G (fourth position)

**We Wish You a Merry Christmas**  All solo parts are in first position

**O Come All Ye Faithful**  All solo parts are in first position

**Dreydl**  All solo parts are in first position

*Dreydl* is the Yiddish word for a wooden top that is used in a traditional Chanukah game.

**Silent Night in G Major**  All solo parts are in first position

**Good King Wenceslas**  Solo Violin and Solo Viola are in first position
Solo Cello shifts to E (second position)

**What Child Is This (Greensleeves)**  Solo Violin and Solo Viola use half position
Solo Cello uses second position on the G string

# O CHANUKAH

**Solo Cello**

Traditional
*Arranged by JOANNE MARTIN*

# ANGELS WE HAVE HEARD ON HIGH

**Solo Cello**

Traditional
*Arranged by JOANNE MARTIN*

# WE THREE KINGS

**Solo Cello**

John H. Hopkins
*Arranged by JOANNE MARTIN*

# SILENT NIGHT
## in D major

**Solo Cello**

Franz Grüber
*Arranged by* JOANNE MARTIN

# WE WISH YOU A MERRY CHRISTMAS

**Solo Cello**

Traditional
*Arranged by JOANNE MARTIN*

# O COME ALL YE FAITHFUL

**Solo Cello**

John Francis Wade
*Arranged by JOANNE MARTIN*

# DREYDL

Traditional
*Arranged by JOANNE MARTIN*

**Solo Cello**

# SILENT NIGHT
## in G major

**Solo Cello**

Franz Grüber
*Arranged by JOANNE MARTIN*

# GOOD KING WENCESLAS

**Solo Cello**

Traditional
*Arranged by JOANNE MARTIN*

# WHAT CHILD IS THIS
### (Greensleeves)

**Solo Cello**

Traditional
*Arranged by JOANNE MARTIN*

*Another great series*
*by Joanne Martin*

# I Can Read Music

These easy-to-read progressive exercises by Joanne Martin develop a student's reading skills one stage at a time, with many repetitions at each stage. *I Can Read Music* is designed as a first note-reading book for students of string instruments who have learned to play using an aural approach, such as the Suzuki Method, or for traditionally taught students who need extra note-reading practice. Its presentation of new ideas is clear enough that it can be used daily at home by quite young children and their parents with the teacher checking progress every week or two.

### Volume 1
- Appropriate for young beginning note-readers
- Level correlates with late Volume 1 through Volume 3 of the Suzuki violin, viola, and cello schools
- Presents pitch and rhythm separately
- Presents notes on all four strings
- Rhythms cover whole notes to sixteenth notes, building on rhythms from Twinkle variations

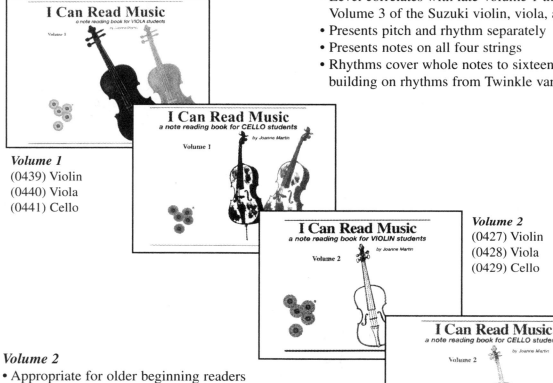

*Volume 1*
(0439) Violin
(0440) Viola
(0441) Cello

*Volume 2*
(0427) Violin
(0428) Viola
(0429) Cello

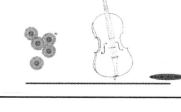

### Volume 2
- Appropriate for older beginning readers
- A continuation from Volume 1 at the Suzuki string school Volumes 2 - 4 level
- Combines pitch and rhythm
- Uses duets throughout, with melodies passing between the two parts
- Reviews concepts from Volume 1 and presents new tonal patterns and rhythms
- Includes time signatures with beats of quarter, half, eighth, and dotted quarter

*Available from your favorite music dealer*

AD2103 0898